Piano

CONCERTO FOR TROMBONE

Commissioned by Case Western Reserve University, Dr. Gary Ciepluch; DePauw University, Craig Pare; Detroit Symphony Civic Wind Ensemble, Dr. Kenneth Thompson; Indiana University, Stephen Pratt; Indiana Wind Symphony, Charles Conrad; Kansas State University, Dr Frank Tracz; Kutztown University, Dr. Jeremy Justeson; Lycoming College, Dr. William S. Ciabattari; Metropolitan Wind Symphony, Lewis Buckley; Missouri University of Science and Technology, Dr. Robert J. Cesario; Purdue University, Jay Gephart; Rock Valley College, Erik Oberg; Texas Christian University, Bobby Francis; University of Arizona, Gregg Hanson; and University of Kansas, Dr. Paul W. Popiel; Walnut Creek Concert Band, Harvey Benstein.

Commission initiated by Daniel Baldwin.

By JAMES A. BECKEL Jr.

HAL•LEONARD® CORPORATION

7777 W. BLUEMOUND RD. P.O. BOX 13819 MILWAUKEE, WI 53213

About the Work

The *Trombone Concerto* was written in the summer of 2013 for a joint commission of ten bands organized by Daniel Baldwin. The performance at DePauw University on October 15, 2013 was the premiere of this work in piano reduction, performed by James Beckel on trombone and Greg Martin on piano. Joseph Alessi premiered the orchestral version of the work on April 5, 2014, with the Gulf Coast Symphony, John Strickler conducting. The band version was premiered on April 29, 2014, with Bill Mathis, soloist, performing with the Detroit Symphony Civic Winds, Dr. Kenneth Thompson conducting.

The bands and their conductors participating in this commission are Case Western Reserve University, Dr. Gary Ciepluch; DePauw University, Craig Pare; Detroit Symphony Civic Winds, Dr. Kenneth Thompson; Indiana University, Stephen Pratt; Indiana Wind Symphony, Charles Conrad; Kansas State University, Dr. Frank Tracz; Kutztown University, Dr. Jeremy Justeson; Lycoming College, Dr. William S. Ciabattari; Metropolitan Wind Symphony, Lewis Buckley; Missouri University of Science and Technology, Dr. Robert J. Cesario; Rock Valley College, Erik Oberg; Texas Christian University, Bobby Francis; University of Arizona, Gregg Hanson; University of Kansas, Dr. Paul W. Popiel; and Walnut Creek Concert Band, Harvey Benstein.

The work is composed in three movements and the first movement begins with a long tutti introduction marked Moderato maestoso. The opening theme, heard in the trombone at the Andante misterioso in the first movement, presents a conflict between the major and minor third. This haunting motif is heard throughout the work and is a unifying theme melodically and harmonically. In this first movement, after the opening Andante misterioso, a rondo-like form continues in a tempo marked Allegro moderato.

While the standard concerto form is made up of three movements, in this concerto, the second movement borrows from the symphonic four-movement form, combining a slow, reflective Andante section with a joyful, waltz-like Allegretto. These two sections are through-composed, acting as one movement. The ending of this movement uses elements from both sections in its conclusion.

The third movement is the most intense of the three, continuing the on-going conflict between major and minor tonality. The haunting opening trombone motif from the first movement returns in the middle of this third movement as if to ask for sanity in a chaotic world. This is followed quickly with a Presto that races to a climactic ending.

This work is less programmatic than most of the composer's body of work. Although the concerto is based on personal reflections and introspections, throughout this work, the composer, at age 65, is looking for answers to life's questions that most people have regarding their existence and the meaning of life. With age comes only the realization that he has more questions than answers to these great religious and philosophical mysteries. The composer decides in his own mind that mankind does have free will, but firmly believes that the consequences of man's free will can also lead to destinies that are unavoidable. This is the programmatic basis for the 3rd movement. The composer further believes that we are capable of being good or bad in the choices that we make throughout our lives. In one regard, this work represents the conflict between good and evil in the real world, religiously and philosophically. In the composer's mind the opening of the second movement is religious in nature and is a search for truth in the world. The scherzo that follows in this second movement loosely reflects the composer's feelings regarding the celebration of life, but as the opening Andante theme now heard in the trombone returns at the end of this movement, against the celebrative theme from the scherzo, now present with major and minor keys being concurrent, the movement ends with questions unanswered.

This concerto is available for band and orchestra accompaniment as well as the piano reduction.

The composer's website: www.jimbeckelmusic.com

About James Beckel, Composer

James Beckel graduated from the Indiana University School of Music and has been the Principal Trombonist with the Indianapolis Symphony since 1969. He is also on the music faculty at DePauw University. In addition to these responsibilities he has been a very active composer and arranger. Hal Leonard Corporation publishes several of his works. He was born in Marion, Ohio in 1948.

Many original works have been performed by several professional orchestras such as Minneapolis, Boston, St. Louis, Atlanta, Houston, Cincinnati, Baltimore, Detroit, Milwaukee, Indianapolis, Rochester, Charlotte, Fort Wayne, Springfield, Evansville, Tampa, Arkansas, Oklahoma City, Phoenix, New Mexico, Chautauqua, Terre Haute, South Bend, Omaha, Knoxville, Delaware, West Virginia, Jacksonville, etc. His works have been broadcast nationwide via television and radio broadcast by groups including the Cincinnati Symphony, the Rochester Philharmonic, the Nashville Symphony, and the U.S. Coast Guard Band.

Beckel's works have been recorded by the Indianapolis Brass Ensemble, the Houston Symphony, and the Indianapolis Symphony. In addition, some of his works for band have been recorded by the Coast Guard Band, the Marine Band, and the DePauw University Band. Greg Hustis and members of the Dallas Symphony recorded *The Glass Bead Game* horn concerto for a CD released in November of 2004 and Velvet Brown recorded *Concerto for Tuba and Percussion*, which was released early in 2007. The Texas Horns recorded a work, *Portraits of the American West*, which was especially commissioned for a CD released in 2008.

Mr. Beckel has received many composition grants. He has been an Individual Arts Fellow through the Indiana Arts Commission and the National Endowment for the Arts, and was one of 50 composers chosen nationwide to be part of the Continental Harmony Project. *Liberty for All* was written for that commission from Composers Forum in 2000 and has been broadcast multiple times on national television with the Nashville Symphony performing. *The Glass Bead Game: Concerto for Horn and Orchestra* was nominated for a Pulitzer Prize. *The Glass Bead Game* was premiered by the Indianapolis Chamber Orchestra on November 10, 1997. Kent Leslie was the horn soloist. *The Glass Bead Game* is now available with orchestra, wind ensemble, piano, and chamber ensemble. The wind ensemble version of this concerto, written in 1999 was nominated for the Grawemeyer Award in that same year and was recorded by the DePauw University Band in 2000.

Liberty for All and another patriotic work entitled *The American Dream* were featured works on a national A&E TV broadcast in the summer of 2003 with the Nashville Symphony Orchestra. Over 27 million people watched that program. The band version of this work was completed in 2002 and the United States Coast Guard Band released 10,000 copies of this work on one of their CD's. Mr. Beckel's *Concerto for Tuba and Percussion* was composed in 2003. One of many performances of this Tuba/Percussion Concerto occurred at the 2004 Indiana MENC Convention in Indianapolis. Another work by Mr. Beckel, *Fantasy after Schubert*, was premiered in September of 2004 by the Indianapolis Symphony with Mario Venzago conducting. It was commissioned for the ISO's 75th anniversary season.

A three-movement *Sonata for Trumpet and Organ* was completed in 2005. Mr. Beckel has also written several works for brass choir and brass quintet. In June of 2006, James completed a commission by the Air Force Band of Flight for a narrated patriotic work entitled *Gardens of Stone*. Later that year, the Indianapolis Chamber Winds performed the world premiere of his work, *Music for Winds, Percussion, and Piano*. And in March of 2007 a world premiere took place with the Indianapolis Symphony, *Toccata for Orchestra*. His *Concerto for Brass and Orchestra* premiered in 2015, also with the Indianapolis Symphony.

A partial catalogue of his works are listed below:

"The Glass Bead Game"	A three movement concerto for horn and orchestra. Also available for band, piano reduction, and chamber ensemble. The piano reduction is published by Hal Leonard Corporation.
"Night Visions"	A four movement programmatic work for orchestra.
"The American Dream"	A patriotic overture written for orchestra. This work is also available for band from Hal Leonard Corporation.
"Waltz of the Animals"	A children's work for orchestra and narrator.
"Celebrations"	A jazz pops overture for orchestra.
"A Christmas Fanfare"	A Christmas overture for orchestra. Also available for brass choir and band.
"Freedoms Hope"	A work for brass quintet and optional percussion.
"Musica Mobilis"	A work for brass choir. (Also available for orchestra.)
"Inaugural Fanfare"	A regal festive work for band.
"Three Sketches for Orchestra"	A three movement work for orchestra featuring jazz trombone soloist.
"Amazing Grace"	An arrangement of this hymn favorite for orchestra.
"Make a Joyful Noise	A lighthearted symphonic overture for chamber orchestra. This work is also available for band.
"Liberty for All"	A patriotic work for symphony orchestra and narrator. This work is also available for band and narrator.
"Concerto for Tuba and Percussion"	A three movement work for three percussion and tuba solo.
"Overture for a New Age"	An upbeat pops overture for symphony orchestra.
"Primitive Modern"	Solo work for horn and recorded synthetic sounds with optional percussion.
"Lament for Two Trombones and Piano"	Recital work for trombone duet and piano.
"Lost Dreams and Rainy Days"	A pops orchestral ballad for tape and orchestra.
"Fantasy after Schubert"	A classical orchestral piece using themes from Schubert's "9th Symphony" and his "Wanderer Fantasy".
"Gardens of Stone"	A patriotic work for band and narrator. This work is also available for symphony orchestra and narrator.
"Music for Winds, Percussion, and Piano"	A three movement work for chamber winds, percussion, and piano.
"Toccata for Orchestra"	A nine to ten minute classical show piece for orchestra.
"Musical Masque (for the Seasons)"	A chamber work for string quartet, percussion, and trombone. Can be played between stanza readings of James Whitcomb Riley's delightful poem, "Masque of the Seasons".
"Symphony for Band"	An 18-minute work in three movements for wind ensemble.
"Fanfare of Honor"	Overture for mid-level band.
"In the Mind's Eye: Images for Horns and Orchestra"	A three movement Konzertstück for horns and orchestra. Also available with band and piano version published by Hal Leonard Corporation.
"Dialogues"	A three-movement chamber work for clarinet, violin, piano, bass and percussion.
"Freedom Tower"	A patriotic work honoring the enduring American spirit.
"Concerto for Brass and Orchestra"	A concerto for full orchestra featuring brass.

CONCERTO FOR TROMBONE

Piano Reduction

(Performance Time:
19 minutes & 45 seconds)

By **JAMES A. BECKEL, Jr.**

Piano Reduction Edited by
Greg Martin and
Sylvia Patterson-Scott

1st Movement

Più mosso poco a poco *(To letter U)*

2nd Movement

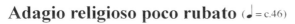

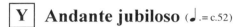

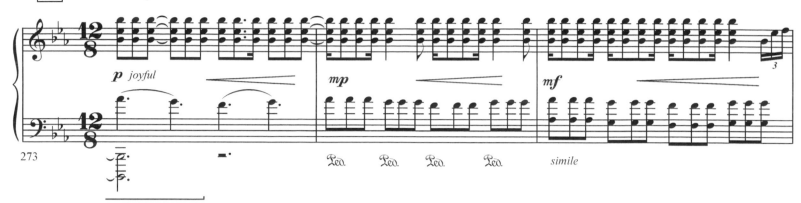

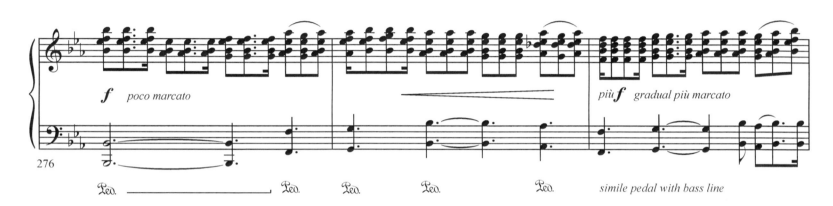

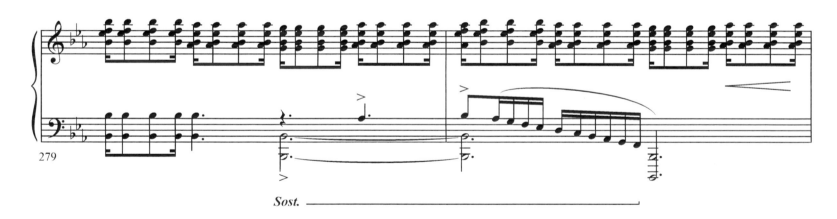

Trombone

CONCERTO FOR TROMBONE

Commissioned by Case Western Reserve University, Dr. Gary Ciepluch; DePauw University, Craig Pare; Detroit Symphony Civic Wind Ensemble, Dr. Kenneth Thompson; Indiana University, Stephen Pratt; Indiana Wind Symphony, Charles Conrad; Kansas State University, Dr Frank Tracz; Kutztown University, Dr. Jeremy Justeson; Lycoming College, Dr. William S. Ciabattari; Metropolitan Wind Symphony, Lewis Buckley; Missouri University of Science and Technology, Dr. Robert J. Cesario; Purdue University, Jay Gephart; Rock Valley College, Erik Oberg; Texas Christian University, Bobby Francis; University of Arizona, Gregg Hanson; and University of Kansas, Dr. Paul W. Popiel; Walnut Creek Concert Band, Harvey Benstein.

Commission initiated by Daniel Baldwin.

By JAMES A. BECKEL Jr.

HAL•LEONARD®
CORPORATION
7777 W. BLUEMOUND RD. P.O. BOX 13819 MILWAUKEE, WI 53213

CONCERTO FOR TROMBONE

Trombone

(Performance Time:
19 minutes & 45 seconds)

By JAMES A. BECKEL, Jr.

1st Movement

* (Alternate positions are only suggestions from the composer.)

2nd Movement

3rd Movement

3rd Movement